Wilderness Lessons

JM Miller

Dear Rachel,
for a magnificently bright being —
I wish you all the blessings, love and
magic a life can offer. Thank you for your deep
wisdoms & heart.
love,
JM Miller

FUTURECYCLE PRESS
www.futurecycle.org

Cover artwork, "flying crow," by Rae Diamond; cover design and author photo by Corinne Manning; interior book design and cover execution by Diane Kistner; Hoefler text with Ocean Sans Extra Bold titling

Library of Congress Control Number: 2016947852

Published by FutureCycle Press
Lexington, Kentucky, USA

ISBN 978-1-942371-08-3

for all the animals who never gendered me

Contents

1. The Lessons

2. Cast

3. Unbetween

4. Under Cleave

No special effort was necessary to cleave
where the cleavage already existed.

—William Carlos Williams

We have to try to cure our faults
by attention and not by will.

—Simone Weil

1.
The Lessons

Wilderness Lessons

I spread my blanket among the scourge
of scattered feathers, a slender bone.

Above, a juvenile eagle whinnies
from a stand of western hemlocks,

clumsily shifting from bough to bough,
fussing his mother from the tangle of branch & mud.

Mother fans her tail, disperses scat like
     silly string
         cascading
into ground's rue.

A few hills over they learn wildness,
howls & guttural moans
intersecting emptiness.

Next to me the sandy-haired boy
burns ants with a looking glass

while a single red ant & I
carry on
with our lives on the earth's surface.

We are all a little wilder under the eyes of eagles
near the gull carcass folded into this light.

March

In the red truck just ahead, a boy's arms hinge
from his rolled-down window. His milky limbs

sever our air like a pocketknife. He flashes symbols
with his fingers, a language I can't make out.

Earlier this morning I stood at the border
between winter & spring;

tree buds marched east to west,
a deciduous army pulling mountains together,

measuring the sun's reach underground:
longing on one side, hope on the other.

I wanted to
hold the world together that way.

My family cat once presented us with a chipmunk,
black & white racing stripes on its back.

He dropped it at my father's feet as if to say *I did this*.
I was killing bees with a birch broom then,

slapping them from zinnias to cement, then
stabbing them to paste, while my father played

war on the base's training ground.
Death teaches us how to love

because we stand in the shadow of its longing, a long
cloud around the planet.

But how to use the lesson?

The boy arches his arms with a bee tongue's precision,
catches my eye. I grip the wheel.

With a smirk, he lowers his rifle,
shoots me dead in the face.

Biscuit

Bury me under the thick malaise
of slick leaves, the unraked heaps of heavy glut
like sticky rice on street curbs.

I want to become putrid with each maple leaf, fusing
into a heap of decay. I've grown weary of puffy coats
& vomit-toned hoodies & humans chewing

in synchronized jaw clicks everything they can get
their hands on. Our jaw sockets are limp rockets,
sweet glands of wisdom tooth misery, gristled conversation.

I want to say nothing
& have you hear me in your heart. I want
your stomach to swell from me, your genitals to shift.

I want to gather around a fire, stretch our bodies over each other,
arm on thigh on belly on back. I want to tear our flesh
from bones, gnash it between my molars, my dear,

swallow the saliva-soaked marrow down my throat
like a wishbone, like a flashlight, a phoenix, a saturated
fairy tale with rich red apples. I want to eat their poison,

sleep well in a box of wood: show is at 8 p.m.,
the grand opening of my annual solo exhibition.
Throw away the empty cup; I am ill with an unknowing.

Am I an androgynous pincushion or
an atomic galaxy of light? An animal with a good ear
or the soup of star stuff?

Have I lit up your sky tonight with my November poem?
I spent my whole biscuit on this
not touching anyone.

Ligature

Hips are parentheses
framing clocks

moving earth's speed

unrelenting balance of
mineral, vegetable, animal
consciousness

I smooth the wet hairs on my legs
like prayer
as if all my love attended this moment
of order

each hair an animal song
a grunt, a howl

each root a sort of ligature
fusing the life I know & the one

behind me, wound time

before the body knew
what it wanted & how to be

Desert Autopsy (2012)

The harbor pulls in, pulls its sheet tight, pulling
    the ground under.

Wintering conifers lean over the banks examining
    barnacle-pendant, seaweed-swimsuit.

I, too, bend my body in the lean
for wild. To walk away from the sea
is to be naked at wartime,
    a gazing body.

I remember the wrecked season, white bone
of drought, fire opening its giant jaws in the west,
gypsy moths spinning cocoons of sorrow.

On the last day of the year, pinyons & junipers are dying.
Fences in Los Alamos still breathe fire.

What is the effect of drought?
    ask the government buildings
    drawing blueprints to save the world

while a pinyon tree simmers in its bark behind a plexi tower.
It shrivels, starves, lets its branches down.

I can't climb this picture, but can you imagine it?
You've seen the pinyon grow, twisting like wet laundry
devoted to the wind sculpting mesa & valley.

I've heard the trees roam at night, calling with their voices.
    What was it, the solemn whisper?
    What calling rubbed the wind, combed the wintering
pencils of grass, laid bare the open spaces? And then I knew

it wasn't for me, not for me on the wind; not for me
were the long shadows, invisible xylem of veins;
not mine the forged silver, fortune of stars.

Army, the poets have arrived; call your horses, call
the cavalry. Lick your feathers, stick them to the dying.

We stand here in the hollowed tree,
language unfolding like children.

Earthworms

I measure minutes in lengths of earthworms,
pink-brown fingertips roiling like waves.
This began when I was a child watching my father

leave at sunrise in pressed BDUs, his shirt cuffs
starched in predetermined folds.
I spent seasons pulling leaves apart at their veins

while men tested cannons on the outskirts of the base.
I licked dew from my fingers, spread the leaf's paste
onto my palm. I asked if worms have souls. I asked

what happens when the worm is pressed into a shoestring.
My heart learned to measure grief in this way:
strips of leaves, reams of veins like floss at my feet.

I learned to hear life's dark echo inside the violin's
cedar cavern as it played on the family phonograph
& measure my father falling inside its history.

Today I am eight states away from this
at a grey spillway in Kansas. A decade after the floodgates
opened, eroded rocks display their horizontal measures

like the tracking of a rolling pulse.
I trace an ice age with my fingertip, its yellow dust
gathering together the unswept story of us.

Field Notes (The Arcade Poem)

For fifty cents you can sharpen a fang,
        sink your claw around the rifle's trigger.

Take cover behind the bush & sidle the plastic butt
        firmly to your shoulder.

Warm sunset drips in the background; breathe
        an arrow down the gun's familiar sight.

A deer hops through the pasture, nibbles oat straw,
        looks straight up the rifle's barrel.

Confess you love the composition, the way
        it eases your senses into a finely tuned fork

banging against flawless crystal.
        Confess you loved that talented seal on TV who gripped

drumsticks, beat "Sweet Caroline" into trash can lids
        in David Letterman's uptown studio.

The seal's name was Henrietta & you wanted to accompany her
        with your bamboo recorder like the solo performance

in the lunchroom when you were ten. All red-faced,
        asphyxiated & wanting to die. We were all dreams then.

Shoot the deer. You shoot the deer, drop the rifle
        & leave the bar. Who knew she'd come prancing out—
        first right to left

then so innocently left to right, begging to be seen.
        The landscape drew you in, made a promise.

You became the animal you were meant to be.

The Reception

We gather under severing fluorescence
around a table softened by the swaddling of cloth
piled with napkins rolled like domesticated pets,
plates layered with docile slabs of ham,
carrot nubs limp as nose tips next to the yawning curve
of celery segments & skewered gherkins
in tedious juice, stale pita points of conversation,
unstimulated wieners censored by crusted bread,
the sesame-studded crackers with perforated impressions,
florets of broccoli the color of aged refrigerators,
heads of cauliflower the color of walls
& submissive cheese cubes hunkered in the platter's shelter.
We gather by the hors d'oeuvres table in our breathing machines,
exchanging oxygen from the stratosphere of prayer, where our animal
hearts loosen their lines into maps of empty spaces like the intimacy
of wind fondling corn stalk, tickling silk strings, sounds that roam
unheard like the grizzly scratching its shoulder in the wild.

Plot

we are alone here in the garden, both
homeless in this moment
    summer's plumb line is a bulbous pit
    inside a belly of veins & tendons

we are strangers here & everywhere
our mantra: I will not harm you

potato root growing potato
    I will not harm you
    kale stalk & radish root snug in bed

we know this poem cannot save silence for us; it is hoax
like cloud cover, like clover, stage clothes, sound bites

these bodies are antennae
    to toothed saws
    & ancient firs that wrap us in their hollows

in the garden plot we
separately watch
spinach unpinch
gather air in its too-free arms

we hear the finch rustling the hedge
the bench, your delicate bed a monk's den at dawn

    I fold the garden hose like a sheet

Worry Dolls

we tell prayers to dolls & bury them
    below pillows like teeth

        where else can wishes go
        but to the ancestral arms of trees
        aspirin of white willow

we need rivers of magic to carry us

        like the tale of the beheaded boy who became a bird
        when his bones were buried under the juniper

on a military base in the 80s
    I twirled with helicopter leaves
    dizzy dervishes, until my mind lost its body

        the big-leaf maple was a bomber in spring
    as I sang *helicopter, helicopter, please come down*

    my bamboo recorder
    my whistling grass
    my rainstick warning

do we learn to see in order to believe or to dream

I ask a city's sagging cathedral of trees
    standing linearly

the bus is a bulging egg carton
    filled with souls & shoes

the buddhist nun in a burgundy robe
    asks the driver a hundred questions of existence

this lousy business of being human
    a tiny box of threaded dolls

I grew up on army bases & am regulated
      to the sounds of friendly fire, blank rounds

          live fire
          had the fire died suddenly

simulated war a form of play just over the fence
      I found my first casing when I was five
          my brother asked if it was worth a quarter

this was shortly before I grew breasts
      I will never forgive myself for that

the root of worry is to strangle or choke
as in a flower coughing dust

          the mother on the bus clutches her baby
      moans that hold the blues in her belly

          the girl practices ballet in the city's window
          as men light pipes through the glass

a man curses with a dagger of feathers
slashes the air's puffed chest

          the figure under the dingy juniper comforter
          who isn't yet a bird
          rustles between doorways

          the ex-soldier sings a poem into a ghost
      dips its ladle deep into paper
the doll strings pull tight into sutras

          sand, paper, twig
          a dead thing for the birds, he writes

god, the seagulls love it here
jesus, I am carcass

Golden Egg

I packed a nature documentary for my nature retreat
    in a bundle of wool socks. I watch

emperor penguins skid like ellipses on their deflated bellies, each
    dragging a species on its heels, a single
        golden egg between its legs.

In the bathroom the splatter of a woman's dead eggs stains the wall,
    her cotton tampon soaked in blood,
        another golden month.

In the cranky refrigerator hollow sounds of a glacier recede
    into hallows distant as the dry cough of a goose
        pinned neatly into this story's pattern

while outside
the forest flings prayer beads into my throat's empty plume—
    19, 20, 21 prayers—& the last raven
        is a whooping monk between day & night.

A coyote mutters with spit jowl; human hunting
    season & deer are ripe with wild thyme
        sprouting in clusters.

Sometimes my eyelids seize under poetry's cleaving whenever a god
    stirs the pot or when a raven
        cracks a nut in its throat.

When was the origin of confession? When did the river stop translating
    the stars? I look to the forest for myth & the
        sleek bone of beak,

the skin of the sea gesturing for the white-flagged boat to set the
    planet free. I once imagined a golden deer
        resting its head on my shoulder, but

what I meant
        was that it saved me the way a story clings
                so closely to life that you walk into it

& wish hard that it may teach us how to live.

2.
Cast

Pileated Woodpecker

stop looking: you can't *make* the body
she said, you *find* it

the woodpecker lowers its head
to the hollow atrophy of a mulberry log
humming a curtain of undertones

a wood beetle folds itself
into an ear
stretches, squats, shifts, swerves

the teacher said you can't define what is always
changing, as my arm traced the model's still
features, chased the ghosts evading through her seams

the way life flies out of us

     is like catching a fly
     with our bare hands

or like the beetle buried inside the echo
of a mossy tunnel

     da da   dum
     da da   dum

beak tapping, the trapping persistence
of the wavering anapest as it hurls its anvil
into the ending

there's death in definitions

as the beak lifts the scurrying beetle
from its nest

& her soul crouches behind her skin
for the next pose.

Plucked

for Aung San Suu Kyi

Behind the turkey a heavy-beaked crane
hovers. Faint sound of an alarm

bleep-bleeps a smoke signal
lost in the dense air above water.

The turkey stands peg-legged in an island
of long grass, boastful red wattle swinging

its nervous pendulum. It is a fugitive
without hands to raise: *I give up.*

I hope it bites. That, if it had to, would maul my arm
until it was a piece of itself. We keep our distance,

exchanging a long look, the silence
before peace or riot.

Just yesterday the turkey was pulled on a string
by four neighborhood kids in denim coats.

They marched the turkey across the road, stood
in a circle, tossed the turkey like a sack.

Because I have sometimes been her, because
I am of her, I begged the stupid bird

to *fly, just fly*
as it struggled in their arms, keeping its mouth shut.

This is what it means to be submerged in dirty water—
forty fingers around your throat.

Sunflower Seeds

after Ai Wei Wei

I've been pinning language to the girl with rain
I've rained on the girl with hands
placed a plant in her cupped palms
I've created a rain girl to show you how
one seed is all seeds, why
a seed is important if it begins in the rain in her hands
how the seed is important for understanding the girl
with long black hair who studies time
against her smock as she works
The rain girl, I will tell you, lives
on the fault line of freedom, a freedom
her mother saw pull away like headlights
& those lines are lineal maps on each of her hands
& our spines which hold us upright burn with ech-
oes of ancestry. See how her

mother's ghost whitens through circuits
flicks memory's switch
reminds her hands to move with cruel elegance
The girl's eyes burn with next year's earthquake
which will settle the cellars like graves
See her paint the cast seed with two black lines
making a sunflower exist
making a sunflower exist
you just put together the parts
you show the girl catching rain in her palms
cupped to gather to assemble collect congregate stockpile
harvest in the cellar of slender eggs
in the damp liturgy of her family gathered in this purpose
I will tell you how she casts her seed in a united heap
like a fishing line for a story in two black lines

Paper Sparrows (At the Museum)

a slip of paper no larger than a dollar
records the scale of value for a slave.

Rows of age & rows of worth, the black
body's gains & losses over time.

You see the paper is degrading, yellowing
tree fibers from an oily thumb nearly enough

to erase the pencil's mark.

At the next exhibit white poets
read paper sparrows to sleep—

a stiff wind in their feathers—still
love in their curated bodies of paper.

They lean in until a black fly in the bird's eye
tires, eating away the carrion into sight,

& they see suddenly a boy,
his invisible hands raised, opening his heart

to a country refusing to remember him.
Some keep the dead alongside them,

feathers in the cap, the bittersweet blues
of fairy tales, while others open & close

the birds' beaks to hear
the price of a spirit, the labor of a body,

a hundred dollars for each year of life,
the value of a dead boy in the street.

The Famous Wolf: A Triolet

She bound wild in a fragile basket   lovely eggs

the famous wolf
we traveled for a glimpse

    though her breath made ghosts
    & legends we won't renege

she bound her wild in a fragile basket   lovely eggs

    holy holy land of the hunt
    holy holy powder keg

    she rolled in fur of the dead
    pushed death in—a recompense

binding her to the wild in a fragile basket   such lovely eggs

the famous wolf
we traveled for a glimpse

Poem Wearing Socks

The cloth puppet detaches from his strings
& walks away,
ratty fibers behind him like coattails.

What if the great questions worked this way?
Changing socks before bed at night.

Each of our steps sweeps the earth, so we
become each other's poems—
hear the train's whistle lasso the air
like a resting boy.

Sometimes I wish I hadn't met the stars so clearly,
cleaved as we are to darkness.

Alphabet

At 7 o'clock the sun's grey wool
is a distant hat.

The sky above the Cascades is a cold forehead
twisting grey lettuce
like snowy sacrament.

> You're learning how to turn syllables over
> like snowballs that
> when stacked on top of each other
> become temples of meaning.

I blame Socrates for this
& pencils
that exact the lessons of fireflies.

> Snow Man, you say
> with the distance of twilight
> clothbound around your tongue.

I see you somewhere
behind this sentence

behind this chicken wire
unfurling a throb of sighs

that is worth everything
when sorrow steps over it.

> Will the grass forgive us
> our bodies of water?

> Such fine thread I barely deserve
> to know this poem.

(Depress the Plunger

on the press, ground down
to what floats above the mesh.
Under iron, the city under
the paper cocoons
of winter wasps
swiping paper houses
with paper bodies.
Hollow cathedral, the earth
holy quiet,
piles of fish
in a bucket.)

Drinking Glass

...because, I ask you, for whom is it meant, the earth, not for
you, I say, is it meant, and not for me—a language, well,
without I and without You, nothing but He, nothing but It,
you understand, and She, nothing but that.
                                        —Paul Celan

the center of earth
is there
without me

faulty milk jug
I chug
the oiled nipple

it's clear we are not wanted to want more here

aquifers cringe
underfoot

& the tired wolf
drags its coat
through thinning snow

pronoun says the planet
is burning

but it has always been
a fireball
catching light

so it is me
who burns with us
on the mother stump

Lullaby

for LP

Hummingbird siphon in persimmon
heavy land

at rain time.

To know your life suddenly
as sleight of hand:

walnut shell
rolling on its hollow black ledges

your seven-year-old voice still
in your throat

in it the sound of a coal train
steaming above the French Broad River.

If we never hear the hummingbird
why do we call it lullaby—

ruby-throated, black-chinned, green-violet ear.

You feel its eyes like old truths
which abandon you noiselessly.

The answer to loneliness is inside the wingbeat:
a vibration calling you to love again.

Cleft

for CBA

Whatever circles our air tonight
moves in sorrow.

Mouth in the clouds, a primordial
silence reaches through,

the cry that wakes up wars, mothers
& land fissures

that open so closely to the planet's core
you can breathe

its heart which drags grief
against her will.

The horse has grazed on clover
this whole day

& wants rest
in this wheeling field

of hawk & straw, tired wisdoms
of reason,

so feed its depths without crisis
& let it home.

The Earth's Memory

When the earth was a child there were no bones.
The wick gathered itself overnight: ash bouquets

at the bottom of flame. There's a song
playing through gaps in the leaves. Now, we

draw our own maps of the world,
ellipses between the poles, small feet of algae.

Mine looks like a myriad of faces, yours
a paper chain holding hands.

A lake stands dormant awaiting
our bodies. If I lie here

will you lie with me? We'll settle
like books on the shelf of mud.

Seaweed blankets us & drought
calcifies our curved spines. The planet

will try to roll us off, oxidized, fossilized,
buried below a dropping bomb,

our ribs counted one at a time.
Let's climb into a cave, scratch into the walls.

3.
Unbetween

Unbetween

after Brenda Hillman

—or, maybe the space between
is what you should give up—
all those edges to consider
with their troublesome beginnings & endings.

(   )

The shoreline seems an edge—

land loses to water

but won't it always be
the place where the water's lid
slips over rock?

Doesn't the land always find its way back
& isn't depth the most accurate measurement?

You once thought that the heart
could unwind from the mind.

(Is it the mind that collects
the losses after the endings?)

How many wishes
in those waters—

Wilderness Recipe (The Ecology Poem)

4 C – microorganism

3 C – insect; butterfly, spider, bee, etc.

2 C – songbird

2 C – fish, trout or salmon preferred

2 C – deer

1 C – diverse mixture of snowshoe hare, fox, raccoon, opossum, short-
tailed weasels, river otter, white-tailed jackrabbit, red squirrel

½ C – elk

¼ C – bison

¼ C – moose

¼ C – each, reptile (bull snake preferred) & amphibian (chorus or
spotted-throat frog preferred)

½ t – bear; grizzly or black

½ t – hawk

¼ t – owl, great horned or screech is preferred, but snowy will work at
higher altitudes

¼ t – coyote

Pinch of eagle; golden or bald

Pinch of grey wolf

Pinch of humans on wilderness retreat (in restricted areas)

Heat planet to 59°F (see directions below for areas with higher pollution).
In a larger frontier, mix glacial lakes, grassy knolls, soggy valleys &
mountain runoff until lumpy. Set aside. In a smaller frontier, sift nutrient-
rich soil, plants (including grass & mushroom), lichen, algae & trees until
mixture resembles a fine powder. Combine the two frontiers, stir
vigorously. Fold in the microorganisms, insects, birds, mammals, reptiles
& amphibians. Spread batter into a biosphere & bake under the sun for an
indeterminate time.

*For areas with higher pollution rates, invasive non-native species or
excessive human population, baking times will vary. Bake in a smaller
frontier under higher heat for a softer wilderness. Test by inserting a
toothpick into the center of the wilderness. When the toothpick comes
out clean, your wilderness is ready to go.

Shadow's Rhetoric

The hemlock's shadow stretches over the park cooling clover & relieving
    grass, into a meadow of resting vertebrae. Two nearly green
        hummingbirds zipper up

& down the colorless horizon flirting the rim. The eagle's nest above
    catches starlight in its pockets. I'd drop a penny,
        make a wish

for wing-air as my last breaths. Here on Levertov's meadow lyric landed
    its grammar, a golden birdcage.

The syntax of my backbone blends
        into phenomena

& I see her there, ink-purple fingertips & a sore thorn from reaching
    deep into the garden

where we all must go if we hope to ever save anything. I pull on
    an extra shirt as the birds settle, flickers & jays calling crosswind
        to their mates. The feeding day over, the glacial slants

of Rainier open to rose, its shadow extending across the Cascades.
    It has done this since times when we looked
        to nest & bird for blessings.

Trees hold their breaths a moment, breaking light into myths,
    a sumptuous rhetoric of us.

Near Fryingpan Creek, WA

Poison-dipped arrows of buttercup & cow parsnip,
the raised eyes

of larkspur & lousewort open singularly
in the Pacific sun.

Huckleberries hibernate tartly for a half-season longer
into the future that may

or may not exist, *the irregular suppletive future participle,*
to be

so far from the straight lines of Seattle & economy
of *to do.*

I nestle my tent between taut mountain hemlocks
to dream the language of stars, a sort of

sequined static laying its fabric along the planet's table.
In this circular consciousness

I feel the clockwise clock of the planet turn over lifetimes,
the Columbian mammoth fossil restless

in its pleisto-static epoch & the long commas
of the Fryingpan Glacier sizzling in their ice coats,

as the loneliness of this body inhabits its skin's
mammalian suit.

I awake knowing that the sun will open Rainier into dawn
again & that I will have been loved

for awhile & the three nutcrackers that whistle
the morning alive will leave me

for another day of feeding from this topography
of conifers & meadows,

piling Mountain ash berries in their nests for a limited future,
theirs.

Orca

Rose dawn flushes our bodies, pink of a spiral shell's inner life & we are
        surprised to be alive
        so uncompromised & budding

a coastline of bodies tangled like kelp in the time of water, incredible
        to remember
        the immensity of water:

the pigeon poop, dust & oil riding the surface streaked by cormorants
        fanning wings of dark tides
        & dinner

& the plunging osprey fulfilling its species' miracle: feathers swimming
        grasping the silver fin of an open-mouthed
        minnow: we all will lose in this.

Eighty-one left of your species & nine here on the shore today
        at Fauntleroy Bay where ferries deliver
        consciousness on a schedule of time

learned from the sun & stars, that ancient vapor stalling in carbon—
        the smell of fuel is not blue, is
        a thick feeling—a swamp

in the bulge of stomach or the intestines bloated with mud from the pie
        that was rich & sweet, too
        good to stop.

In a dream I rode a whale's back, my arms sucked to its blubber, its
        rubber slick
        as drenched kelp—

legless, the velocity of wind wound up in the long spring of its body,
        a hundred yards from shore
        my eyes squeezed against
        ocean spray, my body the ocean

folded us under so wholly, I remembered blue for the first time
        the address of nowhere & knowing
        to memorize it.

No crowd here for this one-ninth of your matrilineal family, *orcinus orca*
        of the Aleutians & San Juans
        seeking the toothpick of Chinook salmon

in these great waters where I rub all the earth's salt on the tenderest joint
        along your dorsal fin & spine
        & you blush rose from my touch;
        I could never do enough.

Return to Nature

Here at the lake, each palm fills & empties;
      the dimpled centers move outward
            toward the water's glassy edges.
Here,
      everything that ever
            happens has already occurred.

The top of the lake eases toward endings
      sinking into submerged weeds that comb & sift
         the planet's losses.

Time on fire like the hot leg of a star
      without meaning, just a burn
         on the cheeks from flushed understanding.

A gaggle of wintering ducks divide floating leaves
      into an expanding V; one tilts a golden light south,
         edges dried upward into a raft. No

thoughts there,
      just velocity dissolving
         to drift.

I take in the air of it, original dust
      tracing each synapse until
         I am

afloat in the dusty immateriality of the lake's surface.
      Closer now, a duck's bill hinges open,
         the dark throat a single O in space.

I offer myself wholly, my former edges
      dissolved & muddy, until I spread outward at the shore,
         decaying sinew grasp-
            ing, releas-
            ing, slipping from me

30 Days Orthodox

My city block is an ornithological daydream,
a field guide fantasy of warbling the worm.

See his orange vest gloss the lips of showers,
the beads of Orion a pin-striped orphrey
cinching his breastbone at its seams.

He is a street whistler, leaf sweeper,
worm wrangler, insect alleviator
wining & dining the unwanted.

See the starlings state their *ffweh, ffwuh*
in evening's sequins above orris root,
flipping leaves like trashcan lids,
doting on the dolorous drumming
of its wings dedicating a ditty to the rain.

See the astute robin, his unaccustomed curiosity
revolving like an orrery around a finger of grass

as green as the viridian choker circumferencing
the pigeon's neck as it pecks cobblestone cracks
to a tune orating from a streetcar.

You can't leash a bird, but you can watch
the silver pigeon spread its tail wings
into an open palm, a crimson diadem flush,
an unexpected flourish unreeling a fury of sunset.

The black-capped chickadee is on a bow with two strings:
one for flight, the other fancy.

Ecstatic sight, the love between us
no fluttering moan or protest but the origami
of a steel guitar sliding across reeds.

Red Poem

A release of dust from above in red,
a thousand sparks of angling light
have me drunk again against this trunk
here on this ground below my red stadium.

I squint, connecting dots one by one,
calico colors mend their crimson fringe,
cobbled edges maple woven wonder,
a blend like being a child again.

A canal of wind shifts the dome;
limb ensembles bang castanet drummings,
a capillary calamity, a twig-twine ditty—
this muse, a music Rimbaud would know:

O let it come, O let it be,
The time of love twixt me and thee.
Such darkness lies under deep piles!
Such spondaic drifts in red leaves!

Leaves march & dangle to the wind's cues
below the camisole trunk, another bouquet
to drop from above, crypt-crossing to periphery,
reaching red light extremity—

Neptune's Glasses

I dip my ear into the earth & pluck
the string of the lake's edge to hear a soul chord
lap minerals with the dry tongue of an angel's palm.

I hear the scuffling heels of gypsies with their long beards
of rope, the wandering women's planet-foreheads like polished rubies
in the clogged forests to the east or like the ancestor waving fox paws
as the guardian of echoes tosses a rattling skeleton in my path.

Or was it like the clay vernacular of human hands at the canoe wall?
Or the striking bison in the magician's cave?
Or was it always the planet's ruby before our senses made sense?

No matter, the ear is an ecstatic wing,
moth dust in a firefly trail spelling the gritty message
of peace letterpressed in yellow magma.

I hear the planet crushing stars on its cheeks
as I let go a little farther into night,

as Saturn wheels its halo like a lasso after love, or as
the separation between the sky & me reveals itself as the white rabbit.

The mold of the singing earth still waits—
you can hear it, yes?

In the birch broom's sweep, in the cedar tree's sweet neck
tilting fistfuls of woven green blankets?

Or in the water's mounting of a stone, the slick release of it?

Or you hear it as the heron pierces the water's sheath,
brandishing itself in the shape of the beak,
the water breaking unevenly around the squirming sea bass
whose puckered lips spit the lake into a hanged man's mirror
arcing like a bridge through the near stars' images.

I see the earth's streams this way: procession of bodies
made heavenly by their star suits,
I wring my body's pond out in the sink & see my history spread

into a reflection of what is now,
into the moment that makes me whole
& here & holy & here & whole & holy.

4.
Under Cleave

The Body of This

The heart is something to follow & it is going
thataway. Rails of iron in the chest

crosshatch the body against the ground.
Throat open to the sky, you'll hear the train coming.

You'll come up coughing tulips, thirsty for sun.
My hot tea bag gave me a message

but I can't get past the smell of dead flowers.
I have added a heaping teaspoon of sugar

& am drinking in death. Overall, it tastes like roses.
My feet were submerged in water as the second hand

stopped its rotation in my secondhand
life of grasping for the red

red skin around the supple seeded pit.
Ancient Egyptians did not believe the heart should leave

the body, that the soul perches there throwing
its pennies into the fountain
            otherwise
                    parched.

                    This way they could always
find their way back.
But trains everywhere seem to be running away

from their tracks, sliding burn marks into grass.
They hum incantatory rhythms with their wheels spinning

like a carousel of white horses walking in circles,
ducking behind sunsets. You see, the base of the petal

spreads its lines outward into fireworks spilling over
the rim. Then there is nowhere to go because its underbelly

turns into something living—an abandoned suitcase
wrapped over & over in fine, white linen.

Salty contents drying shadows around a resting heart
waiting to be struck head-on by something like love.

The Redwood

Desert's dry tongue fills the canyon, sweeps through
redwood's husk lighting its summer windows

into carved pumpkin eyes that slouch
into decaying caves until only slits remain.

The burned trunk is barely a thousand years
of Pacific fog lapping the creek, barely

an echo of the gorged plate of land
flirting its skirt length with an ocean

of want. We make love by the creek,
waterfall submerging the clock, the only stillness

a sharp-shinned hawk that holds time in the cleft
of its talons gripping the sure branch

as I come to the planet for the first time again.
Leaving the creek, the deep shadow of my body

lingers with hers, right there, joining the redwood's
charred figure that mingles the flood of itself.

Equinox

The bus fills with apple slices of sun
on the burnt crest of equinox.

My love is at home lifting the last
golden beet from our tiny plot,

rinsing cool dirt from its roots, setting
aside its greens for dinner.

Here our bodies pinch slightly for balance
as our minds move sluggishly through time,

the hours pushing downward now, tender
rose hips wrinkling into pungent syrup

that leaves a river of stain on our fingers.
It is good to be in this body, scrubbing the planet

from our hands, then reaching for more.
The granite lid over Washington shadows in

from the southwest & we are none the worse
for loving, for losing horizon for so long.

Hunger is neither shame nor enough when
our bodies pull together in stillness.

The Yellow Poem

This is where I fell once. Into a pile
of clementines gathered under a two-legged tree

listening to her wooden gesture of language
which seemed to say *I have only this.*

Sweet peach skin coiled into a basket
of bodies pitted by seed, desire for.

•

The language of nature
          is an old river
navigated between shipwrecks
          & safe landings.
The pier a balcony
          waiting for you with your
glass lamp & suitcase.
          Clouds don't really burn off.
Only, sometimes the sun wins
          when you raise the oily wick.

•

Yellow dandelions hold together the sun.
You fall in love with breathing again.

•

Summer here is overgrown & heavy & I am
the local train passing days. My signals slow

in a traffic of red lights exchanging signals
with the satellites of sun, planet, you.

The absent man with a train driver's cap
clutches a glass bottle in the bend of his arm.

The spout tilts out from the gripped bag
with sweat stains at its base.

He is walking to anywhere & you think
this may be a place you know.

The point isn't that he is drunk,
it's that he is holding on to something.

The battle in the dark bottom he sees
are tiny ships bobbing & sailing.

Battleships on fire, under siege,
all the ladders & life boats.

•

There are places we reach for but cannot touch.
Spaces in the letterpress, where ink

does not sink or show—arches & breasts
around the elegy of symbols.

The ground where all the books about love are
is a mute & solid silence where lake & bed

tangle. I sat in the middle of this road,
the forest around me a levee of arms & legs.

The black segments of ants filed toward a young tree
at the rim of the woods & I watched them twist behind

the buried caves of bark. Wall scratchings torched
dim memories on the wall of fire in the ash.

•

The faint sound of a voice spreads suddenly
behind the trees. Treble of bird & bass of timber,

her tongue describes the silence of grief & sunrise
in a tango of spark.

The symbol here is the gold
flash that finds you in the dark.

This language where I fell once into a raised bed
of supple fire & simple wanting.

•

Lights in paper lanterns are a fleet streaming
between stars. Which is too beautiful to write
through our telescopes of diction & distance.

So is our love, lights burning in jars with holes.
There, I said it.

Of Gods & Ghosts

for CM

You sleep beside me in the car as fog crawls
along the pavement,
turning the road into a rolling sea.

Through the blackest dark a red cross
planted in the ground says *Jesus Saves,*

jams me into the mountain's quartz
like a toothpick between the teeth
or a territory flag from the western frontier.

Last week I watched the sun pour
through the window as you scooped rubies
from the pomegranate.

I loved your hair suddenly & the way
your ancestors stood beside you, apparitions
in our kitchen.

I always reach for ghosts
in the face of your god,
waging mystery as currency.

In these foothills of Appalachia, time walks
with a shortened pace, a tightened grip
on its cloak & cane.

Another sign, *Jesus Spilled his Blood for You.*
A white cloth sails around invisible shoulders

& the pomegranate's
juice drips a scarlet cuff
around your wrist.

I watch your carnival of thoughts in our car
& see out the window a group of children playing
with logs & balls, yellow dogs sniffing their heels.

A deer made of light skips across
the road as a snowy owl lifts.
A fallen hickory spears the sky.

As the Ocean Goes

in our language of nouns
ocean is a field
a looking glass of teacups
dipping into the salty mantle

an object, a mirror & a seer
trying to be
a thirst

the matter   of being
is an unpunctuated geography
a near mythology in our world of stones
that hold the dead in place

what verb shall we call silence
to get the line break right

& who will hear it?

the seer casts & casts   the ground
is fertile enough & a long way
from home

     a fish gathers
     light from every star
     which we are told is always dying

see the fish-being blinking away
what the fish-being knows of water
—no more a mirror than an act

Dandelion

Love followed you into the world like a hymn
inherits the land, shaping the cliffs
where your grandmother stooped low to the planet,
swallowed the sun of dandelions. She passed
that sun to you, golden pollen in your gut.
At night the white moth over your throat unfolds,
our room filled with the silence of dust
as your breath shifts cedar, as ancient pebbles
shuttle through cactus husk. You are suddenly taken
to a dream, a place I can't follow though I curl
into your heart, pressing so close bees sting my skin.
You return to me then, a little further away,
the ancestral soil tugging you toward the dandelion root
that boils bitterly in the face of love.

Prayer Circle

Dead, did I say? There is no death, only a change of worlds.
—Chief Sealth, trans. Jeffrey Smith

The dead have power too.
—Chief Sealth, trans. Henry Smith

Midmorning & the starfall of fog pulling the Puget Sound
like a funeral shawl. We are pinned so close

to this shore that dissolves like spirits just beyond our bodies
swollen with humid hopes. Of the sun

we know little, of a god even less;
the sky has only these dulled corners

& tarnished reflections of itself in a silver lens
left to westward greysong.

Dear ghosts, I see you drink from the stars
of the water's ebb, dipping your palms

low into dust that responds to you, original dust
the blood of ancestors,

dust that holds to the Earth with the sticky love of living.
Just over there, a round of red alders

gestures through whisper-silence, prayer-moan.
I toast the very fog of us.

Late Wind at Puget Sound

Yellow carnations circle Seattle's shores
watching the sun roll under.

A Suquamish woman prays this shore
into shrine, though

a scarf of oil laps the hardened oyster
near her feet that chide
each other on beach rock,

turning over lifetimes & seaweed narrative,
eroded tree roots, discredited algae.

Late wind pushes in from the Sound
& I bend to listen, my spine wholly vulnerable
to animal sky, a long shadow
doubling my life.

The pearly top of the oyster is moon,
diadem for an age.

I wonder what will unearth
when the next god bows down upon this shore.

Archetype on Looking

There was a game my brother & I played
during short summers in Massachusetts.

An adventurous version of hide & seek
where he'd take a head start on his bicycle, pedal to one

of four street corners, draw an arrow into dirt.
The arrow like a compass directing me

to the next four corners of options
where I would find another arrow, eventually, him.

I lean toward the invisible.

Have you not heard
the voices around you straining to speak, not to anyone,
just to pulse from a speaker?

Always an eye on the road behind as if we've all

loaded onto the yellow school bus
for the first time together.

A man at the bar asked, *What is greater than love?*
I stood there twisting receipt paper until it disintegrated,
looked like some desperate collage on tile.

Great love, he said.

And what is greater than that?

Fantastic love.

His eyes wide & bulging, wine turning to vinegar.

What is greater than fantastic love is infinity love, he said,

locking his hands together into two
balanced waves, rocking one-to-the-next
against the bar top.

Love is the pattern running a current through life.
The thread is invisible,

but we keep tugging it like a stubborn splinter.
The arrows my brother drew could not be read, seemed to exist

as archetype, some relief cave drawing pointing
but without direction. Once, a ladybug

landed in the crevice of dirt that signified the arrow's handle;
her rounded red back arched against nothing,

or against me, she was more home than insect inside herself.
My brother's stride longer than mine, even then

as he backpedaled to find me lingering on the roadside
tracing circles around the ladybug, casting a net, reeling it in.

Song

The blackness of our shore drinks the milk
of stars, so the hills are hips slipping into

sequined darkness. My body, my poem
is given to this: undulation of river

sipping stones rolled in air song.
Tomorrow's war & warming sky will wake us

when the first bird strikes his match,
unrolling newspapers like wound tongues,

but here we're held by sap of star stuff,
the shore's rhythmic communion of exchange.

Maybe I say too much of my love
for the Earth, but when the sky

removes its mask from the city's effigies
we all wander back to our thirsty bodies.

Acknowledgments

Ampersand: "Equinox"

Cimarron Review: "The Body of This"

CURA: A Literary Magazine of Art & Action: "Cleft," "The Famous
    Wolf: A Triolet"

Los Angeles Review: "Alphabet"

Poecology: "Field Notes (The Arcade Poem)"

Whitefish Review: "Archetype on Looking"

Written River: A Journal of Eco-Poetics: "30 Days Orthodox,"
    "Pearl," "Prayer Circle"

"Golden Egg" was included in the anthology *Thirty Days: The Best of the
Tupelo Press 30/30 Project's First Year,* ed. Marie Gauthier (Tupelo Press, 2015).

"Poem Wearing Socks" appeared in the chapbook *Cascadia* (Leaf Press,
2015).

"Wilderness Lessons" was awarded the Grand Prize at the Eco-Arts Awards
2014 international contest. "March" (formerly "November"), "Biscuit,"
"Ligature," and "Desert Autopsy" were finalists for *Terrain.org*'s 2013
Poetry Contest.

Deep gratitude to my friends and family who encouraged these poems,
especially Lois Rainwater, Laurin Penland, Erin Sroka, Ashley Hudson,
Rochelle Hurt, Courtney Brummett Alston, Nancy Jooyoun Kim, Regan
Huff and Kate Daniels. An extra thank you to Talia Shalev for helping this
collection find its feet. To my writing mentors, Elizabeth Dodd and Sarah
Messer, thank you for seeing me. To my healing mentors, Ashley Ludman,
Joan Farrenkopf, Cecily Schuler, Tripat Singh, Kristen Hart and JB—thank
you for offering your magic. The students and faculty at the University of
Washington Tacoma have supported me tremendously, as well as Richard
Hugo House, Vermont Studio Center, Virginia Center for the Creative
Arts, the Cabin at Shotpouch Creek and futurecycle press. Rae Diamond,
thank you for your wisdoms, magic and art. To my parents and brother,
thank you for setting such amazing foundations. To the Famous Wolf of
2012, thank you for finding me. This collection would not have been
possible without the incredible love, partnership and vision of Corinne
Manning—thank you for helping me be in the world.

About FutureCycle Press

FutureCycle Press is dedicated to publishing lasting English-language poetry books, chapbooks, and anthologies in both print-on-demand and Kindle ebook formats. Founded in 2007 by long-time independent editor/publishers and partners Diane Kistner and Robert S. King, the press incorporated as a nonprofit in 2012. A number of our editors are distinguished poets and writers in their own right, and we have been actively involved in the small press movement going back to the early seventies.

The FutureCycle Poetry Book Prize and honorarium is awarded annually for the best full-length volume of poetry we publish in a calendar year. Introduced in 2013, our Good Works projects are anthologies devoted to issues of universal significance, with all proceeds donated to a related worthy cause. Our Selected Poems series highlights contemporary poets with a substantial body of work to their credit; with this series we strive to resurrect work that has had limited distribution and is now out of print.

We are dedicated to giving all of the authors we publish the care their work deserves, making our catalog of titles the most diverse and distinguished it can be, and paying forward any earnings to fund more great books.

We've learned a few things about independent publishing over the years. We've also evolved a unique, resilient publishing model that allows us to focus mainly on vetting and preserving for posterity poetry collections of exceptional quality without becoming overwhelmed with bookkeeping and mailing, fundraising activities, or taxing editorial and production "bubbles." To find out more about what we are doing, come see us at www.futurecycle.org.

The FutureCycle Poetry Book Prize

All full-length volumes of poetry published by FutureCycle Press in a given calendar year are considered for the annual FutureCycle Poetry Book Prize. This allows us to consider each submission on its own merits, outside of the context of a contest. Too, the judges see the finished book, which will have benefitted from the beautiful book design and strong editorial gloss we are famous for.

The book ranked the best in judging is announced as the prize-winner in the subsequent year. There is no fixed monetary award; instead, the winning poet receives an honorarium of 20% of the total net royalties from all poetry books and chapbooks the press sold online in the year the winning book was published. The winner is also accorded the honor of being on the panel of judges for the next year's competition; all judges receive copies of all contending books to keep for their personal library.

Made in the USA
San Bernardino, CA
19 August 2016